READY,

STEADY,

PRACTISE!

Rachel Axten-Higgs

Comprehension
Pupil Book Year 6

Features of this book

- Clear explanations and worked examples for each comprehension topic from the KS2 National Curriculum.

- Questions split into three sections that become progressively more challenging:

Warm up

Test yourself

Challenge yourself

- 'How did you do?' checks at the end of each topic for self-evaluation.

- Regular progress tests to assess pupils' understanding and recap on their learning.

- Answers to every question in a pull-out section at the centre of the book.

Contents

Understanding complex texts

To develop as a reader, it is important to read different types of books by different authors from different times and places.

It can be fun to stick with a favourite author but this could mean that you do not learn to understand more **complex texts**. A good starting point is classic fiction – books written long ago that are still popular. Classic fiction reflects its own time, with different customs and the language of the time.

Extract from *The Railway Children* by Edith Nesbit

But father did not seem to be able to get rid of the gentlemen at all quickly.

'I wish we HAD got a moat and a drawbridge,' said Roberta; 'then, when we didn't want people, we could just pull up the drawbridge and no one else could get in. I expect Father will have forgotten about when he was a boy if they stay much longer.'

Mother tried to make the time pass by telling them a new fairy story about a Princess with green eyes, but it was difficult because they could hear the voices of Father and the gentlemen in the Library, and Father's voice sounded louder and different to the voice he generally used to people who came about testimonials and holiday funds.

Then the Library bell rang, and everyone heaved a breath of relief.

'They're going now,' said Phyllis; 'he's rung to have them shown out.'

But instead of showing anybody out, Ruth showed herself in, and she looked queer, the children thought.

'Please'm,' she said, 'the Master wants you to just step into the study. He looks like the dead, mum; I think he's had bad news. You'd best prepare yourself for the worst, 'm – p'raps it's a death in the family or a bank busted or – '

'That'll do, Ruth,' said Mother gently; 'you can go.'

Then Mother went into the Library. There was more talking. Then the bell rang again, and Ruth fetched a cab. The children heard boots go out and down the steps. The cab drove away, and the front door shut. Then Mother came in. Her dear face was as white as her lace collar, and her eyes looked very big and shining. Her mouth looked like just a line of pale red – her lips were thin and not their proper shape at all.

1. What buildings had moats and drawbridges, like Roberta refers to? (1 mark)

2. What did Mother do to try to pass the time? Choose **one** answer from the options below. (1 mark)

   - Told a joke about a princess with green eyes.
   - Told a story about a princess.
   - Cooked the children some dinner.
   - Listened to the voices in the library.

Test yourself

3. Why did everyone 'breathe a sigh of relief' when the library bell rang? (1 mark)

4. Find and copy a simile used in the text and explain why the author has used it. (2 marks)

5. Why does Mother interrupt Ruth by telling her, 'That'll do'? (1 mark)

Challenge yourself

6. How would you describe Ruth? What does this tell you about the time period that the story is set in? (2 marks)

7. From what Roberta says about her father forgetting, what might the family have been talking about before the visitors arrived? (1 mark)

How did you do?

Words in context

To improve your comprehension of texts, you need to read widely and identify words that mean different things in different **contexts**. For example, older fiction uses language from the time it was written, while modern fiction uses modern vocabulary.

For example, **fabulous**:

- used to mean *related to fables*
- now means *wonderful*, *superb* or *very good.*

Even texts from the same era may use words that mean different things according to different contexts.

For example, **wicked:**

- can mean *evil*
- can mean *cool* or *excellent.*

Extract from *Treasure Island* by Robert Louis Stevenson

One of my last thoughts was of the captain, who had so often strode along the beach with his cocked hat, his sabre-cut cheek, and his old brass telescope. Next moment we had turned the corner, and my home was out of sight.

The mail picked us up about dusk at the Royal George on the heath. I was wedged in between Redruth and a stout old gentleman, and in spite of the swift motion and the cold night air, I must have dozed a great deal from the very first, and then slept like a log up hill and down dale through stage after stage; for when I was awakened at last, it was by a punch in the ribs, and I opened my eyes to find that we were standing still before a large building in a city street, and that the day had already broken a long time.

1 In the context of this extract, what does the word 'mail' mean? Choose **one** answer from the options below. (1 mark)

letters   **post**   **coach**   **armour**

2 Explain the meaning of the word 'broken' in the words 'the day had already broken a long time'. (1 mark)

3 Who had a cocked hat? Choose **one** answer from the options below. (1 mark)

Jim   **the captain**   **Redruth**   **George**

4 Where is the Royal George? Choose **one** answer from the options below. (1 mark)

on the heath   **by a large building**   **near his home**

5 What time of day were they travelling and how do you know? (2 marks)

6 The word 'stage' is used in the phrase 'stage after stage'. Write the meaning of the word 'stage' as used in the extract. Give another meaning of the word. (2 marks)

7 Describe the 'cocked hat' that the captain wore. (1 mark)

8 Rewrite the second paragraph of the extract using modern words to replace the older style text (for example: fat instead of 'stout'). (2 marks)

How did you do?

Using evidence from the text

When answering questions, it is important that you back up your answers with **evidence from the text**. This can be done in different ways. Look at these examples of students' writing. They are both ways of giving evidence about the text.

- *The text says the girl pulled a face behind her friend's back, so she is not nice.*

- *The text says, 'Lottie pulled a nasty face behind her friend's back', so we know that she is not being kind to her friend.*

Extract from *The Case of the Missing Stamp* by Dina Anastasio

'Pleasant afternoon,' Fred said, leaning against Sam's old apple tree.

'Sure is,' Sam said, as he placed a flower bulb gently into the soft earth. 'Spring is in the air, all right.'

Fred glanced about him.

'Look at that,' he said. 'What's up there? Looks like a bird is building a nest on your chimney.'

Sam pulled himself to his feet and studied the top of his house. As he watched, a mother bird carried a small piece of straw over to the chimney and wrapped it into her nest.

'Ah yes,' Fred went on. 'Spring is certainly here.'

Sam knelt down and dug into the earth – hard. He wished that Fred would go away and leave him alone. Fred would go on and on about spring and birds and nests and then, just like he always did, he'd start talking about stamps, stamps, stamps. Fred's favourite subject was stamps.

Fred took another deep breath, and walked over to Sam.

'Listen,' Fred said, stepping on Sam's newly planted bulb. 'You didn't happen to see an envelope did you?'

'Not that I can remember. What kind of envelope was it?'

'Just a plain white one. I left it here this morning when I stopped by for tea. My brother sent it to me. It had a rare Churchill stamp on it – cancelled last week.'

'I don't pay much attention to stamps,' Sam muttered.

'Hmmm, I know I had it when I stopped by. As a matter of fact, I'm pretty sure I left it on the kitchen table when we were having tea.'

'Valuable stamp, was it?' Sam asked.

'Very valuable. It is very rare. There was a flaw in the hair. I really need it for my collection.'

'It sounds interesting, but I'm afraid I haven't seen it.'

Fred stepped backwards and turned towards the house, 'You don't mind if I look on the table, do you?' he asked. 'Just in case.'

'Well,' Sam said, 'there's really no point, I did a bit of spring cleaning right after you left, and I'm afraid I threw everything into the fire. If your envelope was there, it's gone now.'

Fred walked towards the door and opened it.

'I know you're lying,' he said…

1 When Fred is talking to Sam, what does he notice on the chimney? (1 mark)

2 What does Fred say is 'certainly here'? Choose **one** answer from the options below. (1 mark)

birds   **spring**   **autumn**   **thieves**

Test yourself

3 What does Sam claim he did after Fred left earlier that morning? How does Fred know he must be lying? (2 marks)

4 Where does Fred say he is 'pretty sure' he left the envelope? Choose **one** answer from the options below. (1 mark)

on the kitchen table   **in the chimney**   **in the flowerbed**   **in the porch**

5 Why do you think Sam wanted to keep the envelope? Explain your answer using evidence from the text. (2 marks)

Challenge yourself

6 What did Fred stand on that would make Sam cross? (1 mark)

7 What did Sam want Fred to think when he said 'it's gone now'? (1 mark)

Characters

Characters play a vital role in any fiction text, and **characterisation** can be quite subtle. For instance, good authors will not simply say that a character is *brave* or *greedy*; instead, they will show the character behaving in ways that make you realise this for yourself.

Extract from *Yacht Rescue*

Lucy banged her bedroom door shut, a little harder than was strictly necessary, and flopped down on her bed. It wasn't fair! They just didn't understand her. Making sure they could hear her anger from downstairs, she kicked the headboard of her bed then sat up, sulkily.

It had been raining for weeks and this was the first really warm, dry evening of spring. Everyone had planned to meet in the park this evening. Most of them would be there already but where was she? Stuck at home, that's where. The worst of it was that Lucy knew she really only had herself to blame. Mum had said she could go, but that she had to be back by seven o'clock. Lucy had complained loudly that was too early, and before she knew what had happened, she had been sent to her room. Once again, her temper had let her down.

Lucy knew her parents would leave her to calm down and she probably wouldn't see them for the rest of the evening. Why keep her here if they weren't even going to spend time with her? She might as well not be here at all!

A thought began to form in Lucy's mind. Her bedroom window looked out onto the flat roof of the kitchen extension below. From there, she knew she could climb down onto the water butt, and down onto the patio. They would never know she had gone!

Wasting no more time, Lucy grabbed a jacket. She was safely on the patio and on her way to the park in a matter of moments.

The route to the park took Lucy along the seafront for a while and she slowed down to take in the view of the sea glistening in the late evening sunshine. Something on the horizon caught her eye. A small yacht bobbed on the sea in the distance. Lucy was no sailor but something about the vessel just didn't look right, even from this distance. Lucy wondered what to do. She had left her mobile phone charging at home, but even if she had it with her, did she really want to alert the coastguard when she wasn't really sure that anything was wrong?

1. What time did Lucy's mum say she had to be back? Choose **one** answer from the options below. (1 mark)

   5.30 pm   **8 pm**   **7 pm**   **6.30 pm**

2. In what order does she climb on these things? Write them in order. (1 mark)

   bedroom window   **water butt**   **patio**   **kitchen extension**

3. Why had Lucy been sent to her room? (1 mark)

4. Write the phrase that shows how long it took Lucy to escape from her room. (1 mark)

5. As well as not wanting to trouble the coastguard if nothing was wrong, why else might Lucy be reluctant to alert anyone? (2 marks)

6. What do you learn about Lucy's personality from this extract? (3 marks)

7. Based on what you know about Lucy, what do you think she might do? Explain your answer fully. (2 marks)

Language and meaning in fiction

When a book is written about life in another culture, the **language** contributes strongly to setting the scene and can help readers learn about that culture. It may be that there are different words used for everyday objects, or that the language spoken by the characters contains some of the authentic language of the culture. For example:

- A novel set in the USA might talk about dimes (small coins), sidewalks (pavements) and bellhops (hotel porters).

- A novel set in India might talk about rupees (coins), ashrams (spiritual retreats) or chai wallahs (sellers of tea).

Extract from *Journey to Jo'burg* by Beverley Naidoo

'Dineo is very ill, Mma,' Naledi spoke between sobs. 'Her fever won't go away. Non and Mmangwane don't want to trouble you, but I told Tiro we must come and bring you home.'

Mma gasped again and held her children more tightly.

'Madam, my little girl is very sick. Can I go home to see her?'

The Madam raised her eyebrows.

'Well Joyce, I can't possibly let you go today. I need you tonight to stay in with Belinda. The Master and I are going to a very important dinner party…'

She paused.

'But I suppose you can go tomorrow.'

'Thank you, Madam.'

'I hope you realize how inconvenient this will be for me. If you are not back in a week, I shall just have to look for another maid, you understand?'

'Yes, Madam.'

The children couldn't follow everything the Madam was saying in English, but her voice sounded annoyed, while Mma spoke so softly. Why does the white lady seem cross with Mma? It's not Mma's fault that Dineo is sick, Naledi thought.

About the author

Beverley Naidoo was born and grew up in South Africa, but she now lives in England. She goes back to South Africa to stay in touch, especially with young people. A teacher for many years, she has a doctorate in education and a number of honorary degrees. *Journey to Jo'burg* was her first children's book. It was an eye-opener for readers worldwide, winning awards, but it was banned in South Africa until 1991.

1 Where do you think this story is set? Choose **one** answer from the options below. (1 mark)

South Africa   **India**   **England**   **USA**

2 What are the names of the mother's three children? (3 marks)

Test yourself

3 What job, as well as writing, did the author do? (1 mark)

4 Give a reason for your answer to question 3, based on the information given. (1 mark)

5 What was surprising about the author's first children's book? (1 mark)

Challenge yourself

6 Why couldn't the children 'follow everything the Madam was saying'? (1 mark)

7 Do you think the author wants us to like 'Madam'? Explain your answer fully using evidence from the text. (3 marks)

8 What do you think 'Mma' means? How do you know this? (2 marks)

How did you do?

An author's use of structure

The **structure** of a text is carefully planned by the author. Fiction texts do not usually have obvious prompts (like sub-headings), however, the author has complete control of the order in which a reader finds out information. For instance, if they want to add a twist or surprise, they hold back information until their chosen moment. This can add to the suspense, interest and understanding of a text for the reader.

Extract from *Jack and the Beanstalk*

Jack was a lazy boy who lived with his mother in the countryside. They did not have much money and what they did have only covered essentials. Jack was too lazy to help his mother or try to earn more money, even though he wanted the latest technology, clothes and music (which they could not afford).

One day Jack's mother decided that their funds were so low they would have to sell their only prize possession: Daisy the cow. She asked Jack to take the cow to market and get the best price he could for her. He refused. She then *told* him to take the cow to market and get the best price for her. He reluctantly got off the sofa, fetched the cow, and set off for market. However, he had not gone far when a small man appeared at his side (he seemed to have come from nowhere). The man offered Jack a pouch of magic beans in exchange for the cow. Jack leapt at the chance as it meant he didn't have to walk all the way to market.

When Jack arrived home his mum was furious. She threw the beans at him (they missed and sailed out of the window). She then sent him to bed with no dinner; partly because she was angry, and partly because she had no food to give him.

The next morning, Jack woke up even later than normal. Normally the daylight eventually woke him up, but today no light at all was shining through the window into his room. Jack could not understand what was happening. He opened his curtains; still no light. He walked into the sitting room and no light was coming in there. He tried to open the front door; it wouldn't move – not even a little bit. Jack's first thought was that his mother was so angry with him that she had locked him in and left. He called her name. She came running into the room shouting about everywhere being dark. He tried the back door and, when it opened, he crept out into the garden holding a bat to defend himself against the aliens that he had assumed had landed on Earth!

He did not expect to see what he did. The biggest, most enormous beanstalk filled the garden, reaching up and through the clouds. Its branches were leaning against the doors and windows preventing them from opening…

1 Which door could Jack not open? Choose **one** answer from the options below.   (1 mark)

trap door   **front door**   **cellar door**   **back door**

2 Write the **two** words that showed how Jack's mother attempted to get him to take the cow to market.   (1 mark)

Test yourself

3 What information does the author give you straight away about Jack?   (2 marks)

4 How does the author build suspense before Jack opens the back door?   (1 mark)

5 What did Jack think had happened that was stopping the doors from opening?   (2 marks)

Challenge yourself

6 In your own words, explain why Jack did not wake up at the usual time.   (2 marks)

7 From the information in this extract, do you think that Jack should have swapped the beans for the cow?
Explain your answer using evidence from the text.   (2 marks)

Extract from *Matilda* by Roald Dahl

The Trunchbull

In the interval, Miss Honey left the classroom and headed straight for the Headmistress's study. She felt wildly excited. She had just met a small girl who possessed, or so it seemed to her, quite extraordinary qualities of brilliance. There had not been time yet to find out exactly how brilliant the child was, but Miss Honey had learnt enough to realise that something had to be done about it as soon as possible. It would be ridiculous to leave a child like that stuck in the bottom form.

Normally Miss Honey was terrified of the Headmistress and kept well away from her, but at this moment she felt ready to take on anybody. She knocked on the door of the dreaded private study. 'Enter!' boomed the deep and dangerous voice of Miss Trunchbull. Miss Honey went in.

Now most head teachers are chosen because they possess a number of fine qualities. They understand children and they have the children's best interests at heart. They are sympathetic. They are fair and they are deeply interested in education. Miss Trunchbull possessed none of these qualities and how she ever got her present job was a mystery.

She was above all a most formidable female. She had once been a famous athlete, and even now the muscles were still clearly in evidence. You could see them in the bull-neck, in the big shoulders, in the thick arms, in the sinewy wrists and in the powerful legs. Looking at her, you got the feeling that this was someone who could bend iron bars and tear telephone directories in half. Her face, I'm afraid, was neither a thing of beauty nor a joy forever. She had an obstinate chin, a cruel mouth and small arrogant eyes.

1 Write the word that shows the Headmistress's office is not a place that Miss Honey wanted to visit. (1 mark)

2 Which parts of Miss Trunchbull's body showed that she had been an athlete? Choose **two** answers from the options below. (1 mark)

face   neck   eyes   arms

3 The word **fair** is used in this extract. Write down **two** different meanings for this word. (2 marks)

4 Does the author want us to like the character of Miss Trunchbull? Explain your answer giving **two** quotes from the text. (3 marks)

5 Explain why Miss Honey felt 'ready to take on anybody'. (2 marks)

6 The author has used the names of the characters to indicate their personalities. Explain what you know about the personalities of Miss Honey and Miss Trunchbull, using evidence from the text. (2 marks)

7 Explain the meaning of the following **two** phrases. (2 marks)

bottom form   present job

8 Explain how the author has structured the third paragraph and why. (3 marks)

9 Do you think Miss Trunchbull will be pleased that Miss Honey has found a brilliant child? Explain your answer using evidence from the text. (3 marks)

10 Write a character description for a character of your choice. This can be based on one you know or one you have made up. Decide whether you want your reader to like the character or not and how you will signal their personality to the reader. (3 marks)

Myths

Myths are ancient stories that often include gods and goddesses, talking animals and other supernatural characters. Myths can serve many purposes, for example:

- they can try to explain how the world was created
- they can try to explain spiritual truths
- they can try to explain the natural world.

Sometimes the word **myth** is used to mean something that is not true. However, many people believe that myths carry a lot of truth. Myths often use symbols. For example, a dove can symbolise hope, or a snake can symbolise evil.

'Remembering Fire' from the Alabama Tribe

Bear owned Fire in the beginning. He and his people carried it with them whenever they went hunting or fishing or searching for honey.

One day, Bear and his people came to a forest, where thousands of acorns had fallen from the oak trees. Bear put Fire down and they started eating these amazingly tasty treats. They could not get enough and wandered deeper into the forest for more, forgetting all about Fire.

For a while Fire burnt happily, but eventually it had nearly run out of food. It died down more and more, until finally it was nearly out. "Feed me!" Fire shouted to Bear. However, Bear and his people were somewhere deep inside the forest and could not hear Fire.

Just then, Man was walking by. "Feed me!" Fire cried out desperately.

"Who are you?" asked Man.

"I am Fire. I give light and heat."

"What do you eat?" Man asked.

"Wood!" Fire shouted.

Man found some sticks and laid them on Fire so they pointed in the four directions – to the North, the West, the South and the East. Fire was delighted and began eating.

Man watched Fire and was pleased by the warmth it gave out and the dancing flames. He pushed the sticks into the centre of Fire as they burnt down, so Fire could keep eating.

After some time, Bear and his people came back to get Fire. Fire was furious and roared with such white heat that Bear and his people were terrified. "I don't know you!" Fire yelled at Bear. Bear and his people backed away. They never carried Fire again. Man does.

1 Who owned Fire at the beginning of the story? Choose **one** answer from the options below. (1 mark)

Man   **Bear**   **Fire**   **the people**

2 In how many directions did Man lay sticks on Fire? Choose **one** answer from the options below. (1 mark)

1   **2**   **3**   **4**

Test yourself

3 Which of the characters could be described as 'supernatural' and why? (2 marks)

4 Why did Fire cry 'desperately' at Man? How did it get in the situation it was in? (2 marks)

5 What do you think is the message of this myth? (1 mark)

6 Where did Bear take fire when they owned it? Name **two**. (1 mark)

Challenge yourself

7 Was Fire right to leave Bear for Man? Explain your answer. (2 marks)

8 The text uses **personification** to bring the fire alive. Find a sentence in the text that shows this. (1 mark)

How did you do?

Shakespeare

Shakespeare wrote his plays about 400 years ago, but he is still considered by many to be the greatest **playwright** who ever lived.

In Shakespeare's plays, characters use old-fashioned language. However, you will often be able to guess what unfamiliar words mean from the rest of the script.

Shakespeare's characters sometimes speak in poetry, and you may begin to appreciate the rhythm and rhyme of the lines when you hear them read aloud.

Extract from *Macbeth* by William Shakespeare

ACT V SCENE VII   *Another part of the field*

Alarums. Enter **Macbeth**.*

MACBETH	They have tied me to a stake; I cannot fly, But, bear-like, I must fight the course. What's he That was not born of woman? Such a one Am I to fear, or none.

*Enter **Young Siward**.*

YOUNG SIWARD	What is thy name?
MACBETH	Thou'lt be afraid to hear it.
YOUNG SIWARD	No; though thou call'st thyself a hotter name Than any is in hell.
MACBETH	My name's Macbeth.
YOUNG SIWARD	The devil himself could not pronounce a title More hateful to mine ear.
MACBETH	No, nor more fearful.
YOUNG SIWARD	Thou liest, abhorred* tyrant; with my sword I'll prove the lie thou speak'st.

*They fight and **Young Siward** is slain.*

MACBETH	Thou wast born of woman But swords I smile at, weapons laugh to scorn, Brandish'd* by man that's of a woman born.

*****Alarums***: an old-fashioned way of writing 'alarms';
abhorred: hated, loathed; **brandish'd**: swung around
in a threatening way.*

1 What is happening in this scene? Choose **one** answer from the options below. (1 mark)

    a battle   **a feast**   **shopping**   **a game**

2 What does Macbeth claim? Choose **one** answer from the options below. (1 mark)

- That he is the greatest king who ever lived.
- That he is not afraid of any man born from a woman.
- That Young Siward is a coward.
- That he is not afraid of hell.

Test yourself

3 What **act** and **scene** is this extract from? Use ordinary numbers rather than the Roman numerals in your answer. (1 mark)

4 In this extract, what kind of information do the stage directions give to the actors? Write down **two** different things. (1 mark)

5 Write the word that is used to show that Siward is killed. (1 mark)

Challenge yourself

6 Does Young Siward enjoy hearing the name Macbeth? Explain your answer using a quotation from the text. (2 marks)

7 Work with a partner to read the script together. Use the stage directions to help you act out the scene for an audience. (2 marks)

How did you do?

Figurative language

Figurative language is language that does not have a literal meaning.

For example, if you describe somebody as a star you do not mean they are literally a star, but that they are very special in some way. The word star is therefore being used figuratively or metaphorically.

Poets use a lot of figurative language, including:

- similes (e.g. she is like a star)
- metaphors (e.g. she is a star)
- hyperbole (e.g. I have a million things to do)
- personification (e.g. the sun is smiling).

'I Wandered Lonely as a Cloud' by William Wordsworth

I wandered lonely as a cloud
That floats on high o'er vales and hills,
When all at once I saw a crowd,
A host, of golden daffodils;
Beside the lake, beneath the trees,
Fluttering and dancing in the breeze.

Continuous as the stars that shine
And twinkle on the milky way,
They stretched in never-ending line
Along the margin of a bay:
Ten thousand saw I at a glance,
Tossing their heads in sprightly dance.

The waves beside them danced; but they
Out-did the sparkling waves in glee:
A poet could not but be gay,
In such a jocund company:
I gazed—and gazed—but little thought
What wealth the show to me had brought:

For oft, when on my couch I lie
In vacant or in pensive mood,
They flash upon that inward eye
Which is the bliss of solitude;
And then my heart with pleasure fills,
And dances with the daffodils.

Answers

Pages 4–5
1. castles (**1 mark**)
2. Told a story about a princess (**1 mark**)
3. They thought the men were ready to be shown out (leave) (**1 mark**)
4. 'Her dear face was as white as her lace collar' or 'Her mouth looked like just a line of pale red' (**1 mark** for quoting either simile); the author is showing the reader how pale Mother has gone to emphasise how bad the news is (**1 mark** for explaining why the author has used the simile)
5. She wants to stop her saying any more in front of the children about what the bad news could be (**1 mark**)
6. Ruth is a servant as she comes when the bell rings and she calls Mother 'mum' (**1 mark**); it tells us that it is set in a time when people in large houses had servants and rang bells to call them (**1 mark**)
7. Father must have been telling them about what he did or what it was like when he was a boy (**1 mark**)

Pages 6–7
1. coach (**1 mark**)
2. The day had already started (i.e. the sun had risen over the horizon) (**1 mark**)
3. the captain (**1 mark**)
4. on the heath (**1 mark**)
5. They were travelling overnight, as they got on the coach at dusk (evening) and he was woken when it was morning (**1 mark** for stating at night; **1 mark** for using evidence from the text)
6. Meaning 1: a point in a journey/process (**1 mark**); meaning 2: a platform where actors perform (**1 mark**)
7. A triangular hat without a brim with points at the front, back and top (e.g. a pirate hat) (**1 mark**)
8. Text should be written in a modern style but contain the same details about what was seen and what happened (max. **2 marks**)

Pages 8–9
1. a bird's nest (**1 mark**)
2. spring (**1 mark**)
3. He says he was spring cleaning and threw everything into the fire (**1 mark**); he couldn't have done this as the bird had made a nest on top of the chimney (**1 mark**)
4. on the kitchen table (**1 mark**)
5. During the conversation Fred tells him that it is a 'rare' and 'valuable' stamp. Sam wants to keep it and sell it to make money, as he is not interested in collecting stamps (**2 marks** for answering that he wants to sell it and for noting that the text tells us it is rare and valuable; **1 mark** only for answering he wants to sell it but omitting evidence from the text)

6. his newly-planted bulb (**1 mark**)
7. the envelope had been burned (**1 mark**)

Pages 10–11
1. 7 pm (**1 mark**)
2. 1) bedroom window 2) kitchen extension 3) water butt 4) patio (**1 mark** for all four in the correct order)
3. she had moaned about having to be back by 7 pm and had had a tantrum (**1 mark**)
4. a matter of moments (**1 mark**)
5. She should not have been out of the house, so she might not want her parents to find out that she has sneaked out (**2 marks** for an answer that links not being allowed out and her parents finding out; **1 mark** for simply stating that she should not have been out of the house)
6. She gets angry quickly and knows it; she sulks; she disobeys her parents; she is observant (she spots the yacht); she likes her own way; she is reckless; and she is inconsiderate (**3 marks** for three or more observations; **2 marks** for two; **1 mark** for one)
7. Predictions should be based on the evidence from her behaviour so far and the means available to her; e.g. Perhaps she will be too selfish to help and will not want her parents to find out she has left the house (**2 marks**)

Pages 12–13
1. South Africa (**1 mark**)
2. Dineo, Naledi and Tiro (**1 mark** for each)
3. teacher (**1 mark**)
4. The author grew up in South Africa, so is writing about the culture she knows about (**1 mark**)
5. it was banned in South Africa until 1991 (**1 mark**)
6. She is speaking in English and they only know a little English (**1 mark**)
7. Example answer: No, because 'Madam' behaves selfishly. She wouldn't let her maid go straight away to see her sick child and she said it was inconvenient (**1 mark** for answering No; **1 mark** for each piece of evidence that supports an answer, whether Yes or No, up to max. of extra **2 marks**)
8. Mum/mother (**1 mark**); text says that she gasped and 'held her children more tightly' (**1 mark**)

Pages 14–15
1. front door (**1 mark**)
2. asked/told (**1 mark** for both correct)
3. That he lives with his mother in the country, does not help her, is poor but too lazy to work and wants the latest things (**2 marks** for three pieces of information; **1 mark** for two pieces of information)
4. The author builds suspense by not saying what it is that is blocking the light, so the reader is left in the dark like Jack (**1 mark**)

5. His mother was so angry with him that she had locked him in (**1 mark**) and left him (**1 mark**)
6. Something was blocking the window so the light could not come in to wake him up as usual (**2 marks** for an answer that links something blocking the window with not waking up at the usual time; **1 mark** for stating that there was no light but without further explanation)
7. Example answers: Yes, because the man said that the beans were magic so they could bring them good luck; No, because they still have no money and now have a giant beanstalk wrapped round their house! (**2 marks** for answers using evidence from the text; **1 mark** for answers with plausible reasoning but which do not use evidence from the text)

Pages 16–17
1. dreaded (**1 mark**)
2. neck/arms (**1 mark** for both correct)
3. treating people equally/light or blonde hair/considerable though not outstanding in size/of weather (fine or dry) (**2 marks**; 1 for each correct definition)
4. No (**1 mark**); e.g. Miss Trunchbull possessed none of these qualities/a formidable female/a cruel mouth/small arrogant eyes (**2 marks**; 1 for each quote that backs up their answer)
5. She knew she had to do something about the brilliant child/she thought Miss Trunchbull would think the same (**2 marks**)
6. Miss Honey – honey is sweet, she sounds sweet and kind, likes children (**1 mark**); Miss Trunchbull – bull-like, ugly, unkind, powerful and may be violent (trunch = truncheon/a weapon) (**1 mark**)
7. bottom form = lowest class (**1 mark**)/present job = current job (**1 mark**)
8. The author has told the reader what head teachers are meant to be like so that he shows the contrast with Miss Trunchbull by then saying she is nothing like this (**3 marks**)
9. No (**1 mark**); she doesn't possess the qualities of normal head teachers, e.g. doesn't understand children, doesn't have children's best interests at heart, not interested in education (**2 marks**; 1 for each correct explanation)
10. These will vary but need to be descriptive and give the reader a sense of whether the character is good or bad (max. **3 marks**)

Pages 18–19
1. Bear (**1 mark**)
2. 4 (**1 mark**)
3. Fire because he is able to talk (**1 mark**), and Bear because he uses Fire (**1 mark**)

4. Fire cried out because it was dying and needed more wood (**1 mark**); Bear had forgotten about Fire (**1 mark**)
5. Many possible answers. For example: Do not take things for granted (Bear took Fire for granted but Man did not) (**1 mark**)
6. Any two of the following: hunting/fishing/searching for honey/forest (**1 mark** for two correct)
7. Yes (**1 mark**), because Bear had not looked after him properly and Man did; if Man had not come along, Fire would have died out (**1 mark**)
8. Fire was delighted and began eating/so Fire could keep eating (**1 mark** for one answer)

Pages 20–21
1. a battle (**1 mark**)
2. That he is not afraid of any man born from a woman (**1 mark**)
3. Act 5 Scene 7 (**1 mark**)
4. Any of the following: Where the action takes place (in a field)/What noises are heard from off-stage (alarums)/When the actors (Macbeth and Siward) enter/What the actors do (they fight and Siward dies) (**1 mark** for two correct answers)
5. slain (**1 mark**)
6. No (**1 mark**), he says, 'The devil himself could not pronounce a title/More hateful to mine ear' (**1 mark**)
7. Check that pupils understand what is happening and pronounce the 'old' language correctly (max. **2 marks**)

Pages 22–23
1. dance (**1 mark**)
2. crowd; host (**1 mark** for both)
3. stars (**1 mark**)
4. his memory/the picture in his head (**1 mark**)
5. All the daffodils together by the lake (**1 mark**)
6. Example answers: 'I wandered lonely as a cloud'/'Continuous as the stars that shine' (**1 mark**)
7. Yes (**1 mark**), because he says that when he pictures them in his mind his 'heart with pleasure fills' (**1 mark** for using evidence from the text)
8. cheerful (**1 mark**); it says the poet was 'gay' (happy) in the company so the company must have been cheerful (**1 mark**)

Pages 24–25
1. It emphasises the colour of the tiger (**1 mark**); and gives a sense of fire/danger (**1 mark**)
2. Each couplet creates a different rhyming sound and they are symmetrical, like the tiger's stripes (**1 mark**); it adds to the powerful structure of the poem, which reflects how powerful the tiger is (**1 mark**)
3. questions (**1 mark**)
4. Who could have made you? (**1 mark**)

5. Was whoever made the tiger pleased with it (**1 mark**), and did they also make the lamb? (**1 mark**)
6. stripes (**1 mark**)
7. Example answer: The poet gives the impression that the tiger is strong and frightening by using words such as 'fearful'. He also wonders about the 'distant deeps' in which the tiger was created, and so gives an impression of how mysterious it is (**1 mark** for stating the impression that the poet gives of the tiger and **1 mark** for backing this up with how it is achieved)
8. Check that pupils are using the rhythm of the poem when reading and adding expression and intonation (max. **3 marks**)

Pages 26–27
1. love (**1 mark**)
2. fog (**1 mark**)
3. 6 (**1 mark**)
4. haiku (**1 mark**)
5. 'like a minnow in a stream' (**1 mark**)
6. BEAU|TY; MOUN|TAINS; O|VER; BLA|ZING (**2 marks** for all correct; **1 mark** for two or three correct)
7. France (**1 mark**), because the French word for five is *cinq* and it has five lines (**1 mark**)
8. 'Beyond the dancing forests' is personification (**1 mark**) because dancing is a human activity (**1 mark**)

Pages 28–29
1. knees; fleas (**1 mark** for each correct word)
2. 5 (**1 mark**)
3. They make the reader laugh as they are humorous (**1 mark**)
4. The first four lines in each poem are written as rhyming couplets (**1 mark**); the last line in each poem rhymes with the first and second lines (**1 mark**)
5. Example answer: There once was a girl named Rose/With long silky hair on her toes (**1 mark** for a word written to rhyme with Rose that makes sense)
6. Individual choices, but a plausible reason should be given; e.g. No, because the rhythm and rhyme are too light and airy (**1 mark**)
7. two mythical creatures, e.g. basilisk/bigfoot/ centaur/Cyclops/dragon/elf/mermaid/unicorn (**1 mark** for two correct creatures)
8. Individual answers but the format should follow the ones on page 28 (max. **2 marks**)

Pages 30–31
1. AABB (**1 mark**)
2. ABAB (**1 mark**)
3. Having to go to bed when it is light (**1 mark**)

4. We should all be happy because the world is full of amazing things (**1 mark**)
5. cream (**1 mark**)
6. sunshine/windy/rain (**2 marks** for three correct; **1 mark** for two correct)
7. Any three words that rhyme with air, e.g. bear/ bare/care/dare (**2 marks** for three correct; **1 mark** for two correct)
8. you (**1 mark**)
9. The poet's own experiences and thoughts (**1 mark**)
10. Children's own two line poems with same rhyme structure as 'Happy Thought' (max. **2 marks**)

Pages 32–33
1. recount text (**1 mark**); it uses chronological order and has a brief introduction and conclusion (**1 mark**)
2. It needs an introduction at the beginning to let the reader know who went, when and why (**1 mark**)
3. Long Gallery (**1 mark**)
4. They were radio-controlled (**1 mark**)
5. 'Apparently' (**1 mark**)
6. She had given him tuna sandwiches/she had given him his sister's sandwiches (**1 mark**)
7. it was successful from the student's point of view because they had fun playing and shopping. It was probably not so successful from the teacher's point of view because the student does not seem to have learnt very much or have been interested in much of the house (**1 mark** for identifying the student had fun; **1 mark** for suggesting the teacher may have had a different opinion; **1 mark** for using evidence from the text)
8. Individual answers but children should write more about the pictures and the visit to the house, rather than the lunch, play and shop visit (max. **3 marks**)

Pages 34–35
1. Put a brick in the cistern (**1 mark**)
2. 20 (**1 mark**)
3. It is wrong to waste water (**1 mark**) He says 'water is a precious commodity'/he is trying to persuade people not to waste water/emotive language to make readers feel guilty (**1 mark** for one reason)
4. Wash them in a bowl rather than under a running tap (**1 mark**)
5. Turn the tap off when brushing (**1 mark**)
6. Example answers: So that there is enough water to go around/So that we can continue to live comfortably (**1 mark** for a plausible reason)
7. Many possible answers; e.g. 'How about washing up instead of using the dishwasher?' (**1 mark**); effect is to make the reader think about their own use of water (**1 mark**)

Answers

8. 'We should be ashamed of such waste, as water is a very precious commodity' (**1 mark**)

Pages 36–37
1. experience/skill (**1 mark** for both correct)
2. online; over the phone (**1 mark** for both correct)
3. Example answers: unique/exciting/fun-packed; makes the reader think that the activities are exciting and encourages them to take part (**1 mark** for identifying a correct adjective; **1 mark** for a suitable explanation of the effect)
4. mid-air jumps; speedy zips (**1 mark** for each)
5. Example answer: A high-wire adventure in the trees (**1 mark**)
6. no lights/too dark to see/not safe (**2 marks** for two correct; **1 mark** for one correct)
7. Answers must be backed up with evidence from the text (**2 marks** for a detailed answer using evidence from the text; **1 mark** for an answer without using evidence from the text)
8. It says it is 'the perfect day out for the whole family' but later it says, 'Everyone aged 6+ can come', so if your family includes children under the age of 6, (**1 mark**) not all your family could take part (**1 mark**)

Pages 38–39
1. Parents can contact their children; Children can communicate freely (**1 mark** for both)
2. 80% (**1 mark**)
3. Individual answers backed up with information from the text as well as own arguments if relevant (**2 marks** for complete answer; **1 mark** for argument but not backed up)
4. People have very different opinions on this matter, so the debate will not be concluded any time soon (**1 mark**)
5. a high proportion are thefts of mobile phones (**1 mark**)
6. Any plausible argument; e.g. Smartphones could be used to do research in class and to make notes (**1 mark**)
7. Author implies that even if schools set rules, parents and children often break them, so even if the school says children are not allowed to bring their phones, the children may still bring them (**2 marks** for a correct explanation specific to the text; **1 mark** for a correct explanation but not specific to the text)

Pages 40–41
1. Education Department (**1 mark**)
2. No (**1 mark**); plan does not interfere with any public or private access (**1 mark**)
3. Mr Grieves (**1 mark**)
4. continue (**1 mark**)
5. Not yet (**1 mark**); Planning Department is 'in favour' but needs Mr Grieves to 'clarify the drawings' (**1 mark** for using the text to explain)
6. Plans were sent to the wrong address, were handwritten (so difficult to read) and needed to be checked by the county architects (**2 marks** for two reasons; **1 mark** for one)
7. Architect's plans need to be sent to the Planning Department (**1 mark**), which needs to check them and issue a ticket of certification (**1 mark**)

Pages 42–43
1. Answers will vary but should be from article: reading/knowledge/writing/comprehension (**1 mark**)
2. discussion (**1 mark**); it discusses an issue, giving both sides of the argument (**1 mark**)
3. Answers will vary but should be from article: improve their reading and writing/stay in touch with family/improved knowledge/global citizens (**1 mark**)
4. Answers will vary but should be from article: see bad things/dangerous online world/forget how to play/spending less time with family and friends (**1 mark**)
5. vital (**1 mark**)
6. Parents and teachers can check books (**1 mark**); it is not as easy to check what children are reading and accessing on the Internet (**1 mark**)
7. Paragraph 2 = Benefits of technology; Paragraph 3 = Disadvantages of technology; Paragraph 4 = Summary of the two arguments (**2 marks** for all correct; **1 mark** for two correct)
8. Children who use the Internet can find out more about the wider world (**1 mark**); if they spend too long on the Internet they don't spend as much time with their friends and families (**1 mark**)
9. Yes (**1 mark**); in moderation/not too much or too often/parents and teachers need to check children are safe (**2 marks**; 1 for each)
10. Individual answers, ideas need to be based on the text and correlate with their chosen answer (max. **3 marks**)

1 Which verb does Wordsworth use several times to personify the daffodils? (1 mark)

2 Which nouns in the first stanza make the daffodils seem like a group of people? (1 mark)

3 What 'twinkle on the milky way'? Choose **one** answer from the options below. (1 mark)

daffodils **trees** **stars** **waves**

Test yourself

4 What does Wordsworth mean by his 'inward eye'? (1 mark)

5 What was the 'crowd' that Wordsworth writes about? (1 mark)

6 Quote a simile that is used in this poem. (1 mark)

Challenge yourself

7 Does Wordsworth like the daffodils? How do you know? (2 marks)

8 Using the context of the poem, what do you think 'jocund' means? Explain your answer. (2 marks)

How did you do?

The sound of poetry

How a poem **sounds** is very important. Some poems are written to be read aloud, and even poems that are just written to be read make a sound in your mind as you read. Some of the most common techniques poets use to create sound effects in their writing are:

- rhyme (e.g. fat cat)
- rhythm (the beat you can hear in the words)
- repetition (repeating a word)
- alliteration (e.g. creeping cat, massive mountain).

'The Tiger' by William Blake

I

Tiger! Tiger! burning bright
In the forests of the night,
What immortal hand or eye
Could frame thy fearful symmetry?

II

In what distant deeps or skies
Burnt the fire of thine eyes?
On what wings dare he aspire?
What the hand, dare seize the fire?

III

And what shoulder, and what art
Could twist the sinews of thy heart?
And when thy heart began to beat,
What dread hand? and what dread feet?

IV

What the hammer? what the chain?
In what furnace was thy brain?
What the anvil? what dread grasp
Dare its deadly terrors clasp?

V

When the stars threw down their spears,
And water'd heaven with their tears,
Did he smile his work to see?
Did he who made the lamb make thee?

VI

Tiger! Tiger! burning bright
In the forests of the night,
What immortal hand or eye
Dare frame thy fearful symmetry?

1 'Burning bright' is an example of alliteration. What effect does this create? (2 marks)

2 Rhyming couplets are used throughout this poem. What effect does this have on the poem's structure and message? (2 marks)

3 What sentence type is repeated throughout the poem? Choose **one** answer from the options below. (1 mark)

questions   **statements**   **exclamations**   **commands**

4 In the first stanza, the speaker is asking who could 'frame thy fearful symmetry?' What would be a simple way of asking this question? (1 mark)

5 Explain what the poet is saying in the last two lines of stanza V. (2 marks)

6 Which part of the tiger could the 'symmetry' refer to? Choose **one** answer from the options below. (1 mark)

claws   **nose**   **stripes**   **growl**

7 What impression does the poet give of the tiger and which words and phrases create this effect? (2 marks)

8 Read the poem in your head and practise the rhythm. Read it aloud to a partner, ensuring your delivery shows how powerful the tiger is. (3 marks)

How did you do?

Forms of poetry

There are many different **forms** of poetry, often reflecting different times and cultures. Many of them have particular structures that the poet is expected to follow. An English sonnet, for example, has the following key features:

- 14 lines
- 10 syllables to a line
- often about love
- often finish with an unexpected twist.

As you develop as a reader, it is important that you read a wide range of poetry, so that you can identify poetry in different forms.

Haiku

Haikus originate in Japan. They have just three lines, are about nature and often contrast two things. Traditionally they have a syllable count of 5 / 7 / 5, but more recently they follow the idea that they are to be "expressed in one breath".

Fog in the air

lost

nature's beauty

Cinquain

Cinquains have five lines (*cinq* means "five" in French). The syllable pattern is 2 / 4 / 6 / 8 / 2.

Cool breeze,

Sparkling water,

Sun blazing on my back.

**Golden sand between
my warm toes...**

the beach.

Tanka

Tankas are Japanese. They contain five lines with a syllable pattern of 5 / 7 / 5 / 7 / 7. They usually contain similes, metaphors or personification.

Over the mountains,

beyond the dancing forests.

The happy child swims,

in the sparkling cool water;

like a minnow in a stream.

1 What is an English sonnet usually about? (1 mark)

2 What has made nature's beauty disappear in the **haiku**? (1 mark)

Test yourself

3 How many syllables are there in the third line of a **cinquain**?
Choose **one** answer from the options below. (1 mark)

    4   **2**   **6**   **8**

4 Which type of poem often contrasts two ideas in nature?
Choose **one** answer from the options below. (1 mark)

    tanka   **haiku**   **cinquain**   **sonnet**

5 Quote the simile that has been used in the **tanka**. (1 mark)

6 Divide the following words into their syllables using small vertical lines. (2 marks)

    B E A U T Y   M O U N T A I N S

    O V E R   B L A Z I N G

Challenge yourself

7 Which country do you think the name **cinquain** came from?
Explain why you think this. (2 marks)

8 Which line contains personification in the **tanka** poem?
Why is it personification? (2 marks)

How did you do?

Structure and meaning of poetry

Different types of poems, with their different **structures**, tend to suit different topics. For example:

- **Odes** and **sonnets** are suited to dealing seriously with topics such as love, death, truth, etc.

- **Haikus** and **cinquains** are very effective for making brief observations about nature.

- **Limericks** make effective use of rhythm and rhyme when a poet wants to make you laugh.

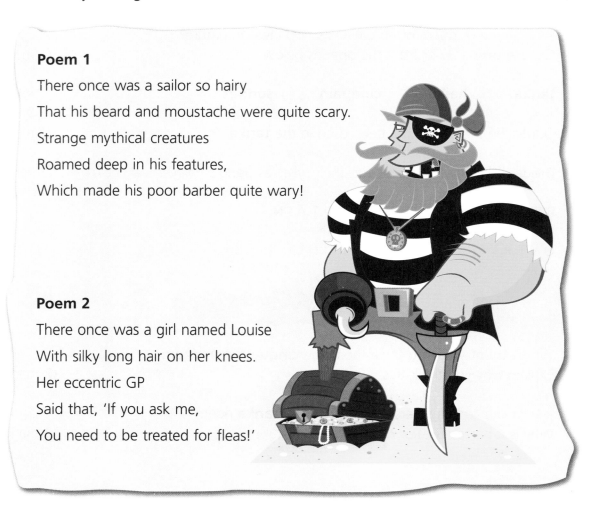

Poem 1

There once was a sailor so hairy

That his beard and moustache were quite scary.

Strange mythical creatures

Roamed deep in his features,

Which made his poor barber quite wary!

Poem 2

There once was a girl named Louise

With silky long hair on her knees.

Her eccentric GP

Said that, 'If you ask me,

You need to be treated for fleas!'

Warm up

1 Which **two** words are used to rhyme with 'Louise'? (2 marks)

2 How many lines are there in each poem? (1 mark)

Test yourself

3 What is the effect of the last line in each poem? (1 mark)

4 What do you notice about the rhyme patterns? (2 marks)

5 Write the first **two** lines of a poem, based on **Poem 2**, where the girl is called Rose instead of Louise. (1 mark)

6 Do you think you could write something serious using the structure used in these poems? Explain your answer. (1 mark)

Challenge yourself

7 Name **two** mythical creatures that the barber might have found in the sailor's beard. (1 mark)

8 Write your own humorous poem in the same style as the two on page 28. (2 marks)

How did you do?

Poetry by Robert Louis Stevenson

'Bed in Summer'

In Winter I get up at night
And dress by yellow candle light.
In Summer, quite the other way,
I have to go to bed by day.

I have to go to bed and see
The birds still hopping on the tree,
Or hear the grown-up people's feet
Still going past me in the street.

And does it not seem hard to you,
When all the sky is clear and blue,
And I should like so much to play,
To have to go to bed by day?

'Happy Thought'

The world is so full of a number of things,
I'm sure we should be as happy as kings.

'The Cow'

The friendly cow, all red and white,
I love with all my heart:
She gives me cream with all her might,
To eat with apple tart.

She wanders lowing here and there,
And yet she cannot stray,
All in the pleasant open air,
The pleasant light of day;

And blown by all the winds that pass
And wet with all the showers,
She walks among the meadow grass
And eats the meadow flowers.

1 What is the rhyme structure in 'Bed in Summer'? Choose **one** answer from the options below. (1 mark)

AABB   **ABAB**   **ABBA**   **no rhyming**

2 What is the rhyme structure in 'The Cow'? Choose **one** answer from the options below. (1 mark)

AABB   **ABAB**   **ABBA**   **no rhyming**

3 What is the poet moaning about in 'Bed in Summer'? Choose **one** answer from the options below. (1 mark)

- Having to go to bed when it is dark
- Having to listen to birds singing in trees
- Having to go to bed when it is light
- Having to dress by candlelight

4 Write **one** short sentence to summarise the author's thought in 'Happy Thought'. (1 mark)

5 What does the cow give to the poet in 'The Cow'? (1 mark)

6 Write down **three** different types of weather that are mentioned in 'The Cow'. (2 marks)

7 Write three words that rhyme with **air**. (2 marks)

8 Write the word the poet uses in 'Bed in Summer' to talk directly to his audience. (1 mark)

9 Look at the three poems written by the same poet. What is the common theme? Choose **one** answer from the options below. (1 mark)

- The weather
- The poet's own experiences and thoughts
- The poet's family
- The natural world

10 Write your own two-line poem, using 'Happy Thought' as an example. (2 marks)

Score ◯ /13

Structure and meaning of non-fiction

The way in which a non-fiction text is **structured** is determined by the type of text that it is. The main text types have features that help determine the structure.

For example:

- **Recount texts** have an introduction followed by a description of events in a chronological order.

- **Report texts** have an introduction, key points and a conclusion, but do not have to be organised in chronological order.

Both of these types of text will normally use paragraphs to organise the information and make it easier to read.

Our visit to Montacute House and Gardens

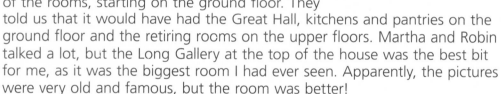

When we arrived, the coach had to drive along a very long driveway (just like it had been in Elizabethan times), so we got a really great view of the enormous house. The coach parked in front of the house and two guides met us. Their names were Martha and Robin. They took us into the house and through each of the rooms, starting on the ground floor. They told us that it would have had the Great Hall, kitchens and pantries on the ground floor and the retiring rooms on the upper floors. Martha and Robin talked a lot, but the Long Gallery at the top of the house was the best bit for me, as it was the biggest room I had ever seen. Apparently, the pictures were very old and famous, but the room was better!

After we had finished in the house, we had lunch. We all sat in the gardens at the back of the house as it was a sunny day. I was a bit fed up because my mum had accidentally put my sister's sandwiches in my lunch bag (tuna – yuck!), so I didn't eat them. We were then allowed to play for 15 minutes and had great fun as there was a huge tree swing that two of us could go on at once (Spencer was too scared to have a go though!).

When we had finished playing, we were taken on a tour of the gardens which were huge (I wish that my garden was that big!). There was so much grass that they had radio-controlled lawnmowers!

After the tour of the gardens, we went to the shop to spend our £5. I bought a really cool wooden ruler with all the kings and queens of England on it as well as a bag of sweets. Then, after everyone had been to the toilet, we got on the coach to go back to school.

I really enjoyed the visit, especially playing on the swing and spending my money in the shop. I hope we get to go on lots more school visits!

1 What type of text is this and how do you know? (2 marks)

2 What might be added to the beginning of the text to make it better? (1 mark)

Test yourself

3 Which room has never been on the ground floor? Choose **one** answer from the options below. (1 mark)

pantry   **Great Hall**   **Long Gallery**   **kitchen**

4 What was unusual about the lawnmowers? (1 mark)

5 Which word shows that the author was not especially impressed that the pictures were old and famous? (1 mark)

6 Why was the author unhappy with his mum? (1 mark)

Challenge yourself

7 Do you think the visit was successful from *both* the student's and the teacher's point of view? Use evidence from the text to back up your answer. (3 marks)

8 Write a recount of the school visit as if the teacher had written it. Think about the things that the teacher might focus on about the visit. (3 marks)

How did you do?

The type of **language** used in texts is often determined by the audience and purpose of the text. For instance, a description of a chemistry experiment will have scientific language, which will assume a knowledge of chemistry.

A persuasive text, on the other hand, may contain emotive language or rhetorical questions to make the reader come to the same conclusions as the author.

Saving Water

Water is essential for life: to drink, to cook, to clean and so on. However, there is a limited supply of water on our planet. Each day, more people are being born and so the supply has to be shared among more people. We also expect a higher standard of living now, which demands a greater

supply of water for use in industries and households. In fact, at home the average person uses **4500 litres** of water a year! We should be ashamed of such waste, as water is a very precious commodity.

Do you waste water at home?

How do you use water at home? Look at these facts and think about how you are contributing to wasting water:

* It takes 9 litres of water to flush the toilet each time.
* A dishwasher (on average) uses 40 litres of water each time it runs.
* Having a bath uses about 80 litres of water.
* A running tap uses over 6 litres of water per minute.

What can you do?

Think about putting a brick in the cistern of your toilet which will take up space so that there is less water to flush each time. How about washing up instead of using the dishwasher? A shower uses only 20 litres of water – why not shower rather than bathe? How often do you leave the tap running when you are brushing your teeth, washing vegetables or washing your hands? Why not turn it off while you are brushing your teeth, wash your vegetables in a bowl and half fill the sink with water to wash your hands? These are only a very few tips that would help to save water – there are many more. Why not do some research yourself about how water is wasted, so that you can be **WATER-FRIENDLY**? We need to think about it today; tomorrow is not good enough if we really value our natural resources.

1 How can you save water when flushing the toilet? (1 mark)

2 How many litres of water are used during a shower? Choose **one** answer
from the options below. (1 mark)

20   80   40   6

Test yourself

3 What does the author of this text think about wasting water?
Explain your answer. (2 marks)

4 How could you save water when washing vegetables? (1 mark)

5 How could you save water when cleaning your teeth? (1 mark)

6 Why do we need to save water? (1 mark)

Challenge yourself

7 A rhetorical question is a question that the reader is not expected to answer.
Write down **one** example of this from the text. What effect is it meant to
have on the reader? (2 marks)

8 Write down the sentence that uses very emotive language in the first paragraph.
(1 mark)

Evidence from the text

It is important that you back up your answers with **evidence from the text**. Sometimes, you might use a direct quotation to do this.

For example, if you are commenting on a text about the health benefits of fruit, you might say:

The text tells us that oranges are full of vitamin C, so they are very healthy.

Alternatively, you could express the same information using a direct quotation:

The text says 'oranges contain a lot of vitamin C', so they are very healthy.

Treetops Fun

Join us at Treetops Fun for a unique, exciting and fun-packed experience. Our awesome High Ropes Course contains over 80 exciting obstacles. Different heights and different challenges for different abilities make it the perfect day out for the whole family! Amaze yourself as you tackle the challenges head on, from mid-air jumps to speedy zips. You'll swing through them all!

You do not need to be a climber or an abseiler. You don't need to be superman. Absolutely NO experience or skill is required for this activity, just a willingness to have a great adventure! The instructors train you, connect you to the course and then you are off!

Everyone aged 6+ can come and enjoy the fun! Children can do the course on their own with parents watching.

Birthday Fun!

How about having the most awesome birthday party ever? Book a treetop adventure for you and your friends. We cater for parties of adults and children. Please telephone for further details.

Booking

You can book online or by telephone (number and website address on back of leaflet).

Opening times

We are open all year round (except Christmas Day) between 9am and 5pm. Why not give it a go and conquer some of the biggest, most fun challenges of your life?

1. What do you *not* need to have to take part? Choose **two** answers from the options below. (1 mark)

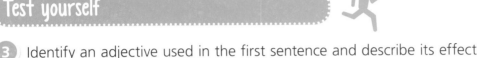

   experience   **willingness for fun**   **skill**   **love of fun**

2. How can you book your adventure? (1 mark)

3. Identify an adjective used in the first sentence and describe its effect on the reader. (2 marks)

4. What **two** challenges are mentioned in the first paragraph? (2 marks)

5. In your own words, explain what the leaflet is advertising. (1 mark)

6. Why do you think the Treetops adventure is not open at night? Give **two** reasons. (2 marks)

7. Would you want to go with your whole family? Explain your reasons clearly, using evidence from the leaflet. (2 marks)

8. Can the whole family go on the course? Explain your answer using direct quotations from the text. (2 marks)

How did you do?

Justifying opinions

When reading non-fiction texts, particularly discussion texts, you are faced with different opinions about issues. It is up to you as the reader to decide what you believe, but you need to be able to **justify** your opinions.

This could mean using arguments made in the text to support your opinion, or it could mean using your own arguments (which the author may not have considered).

Should mobile phones be allowed in schools?

There has been a huge increase in the number of new communication technologies available in the last few years. This, of course, includes mobile phones. In fact, it is estimated that over 80% of young people aged 10–14 now own their own phone. Following a number of instances of phones being used inappropriately in schools, there has been a great deal of debate in the press as to whether pupils should be allowed to take their mobile phones into school.

There are undeniably positive benefits in children being able to communicate freely. Parents like to know that their child is safe and can contact them if necessary, and mobile phones cater to this. Because of them, parents feel they can give their children more independence, allowing their children, for instance, to travel to and from school on their own, which can have its own hazards.

Schools, on the other hand, argue that carrying a mobile phone could make a child more vulnerable to being mugged, both on the journeys to and from school and in the playground. This is backed up by police figures that show a high proportion of crimes committed against young people involve thefts of mobile phones. A further concern voiced by schools is that mobile phones can create a competitive atmosphere, making some children, who do not own the "best model" or perhaps do not own a phone at all, feel left out. The final (and possibly most important) argument against mobile phones, is that they are used in class and distract from learning.

The debate remains open and will continue to do so for the foreseeable future. Meanwhile, it is up to individual schools to set the rules as they see fit, and parents/children to break them as they see fit!

1 Which of these are arguments for allowing phones in schools?
Choose **two** answers from the options below. (1 mark)

- Parents can contact their children.

- Children can communicate freely.

- Children are more likely to be mugged.

- Mobile phones distract from learning.

2 What percentage of children aged 10–14 are estimated to own mobile phones?
Choose **one** answer from the options below. (1 mark)

70%   **80%**   **60%**   **85%**

3 Which side of the argument do you agree with, and why? (2 marks)

4 Why is it likely the argument will continue to be debated in the future? (1 mark)

5 What do the police figures show about crimes against young people? (1 mark)

6 Write another argument to add to the paragraph about why phones should
be allowed in schools, thinking carefully about another use for them. (1 mark)

7 What does the author imply in the words 'and parents/children to break
them as they see fit' and how does this relate to the phone issue? (2 marks)

How did you do?

Summarising ideas

Being able to **summarise** the ideas in a text is an important skill, especially when a text is very long and contains a lot of information. If you can summarise the information, it will mean you can remember the key points more easily and make use of them. For example:

- If you have a long list of instructions, you might summarise them into a short to-do list.
- If you are going on holiday, you might read through a travel guide and summarise which attractions are really worth seeing, or the phrases that will be really useful.

Planning Department

County Hall
Mudgeley MT4 8QT

15 Bart Terrace
Mudgeley MT8 4BE

20th December

Dear Mr Grieves,

We are writing in response to the plans you submitted to our offices on 15th November this year regarding your proposed extension. Firstly, we apologise for the delay in writing but the address that you sent the letter to was in fact our Education Department, rather than our Planning Department. The plans that you sent were difficult to read due to their handwritten nature, and we also had to take advice from our county architects.

However, we are now able to offer you a response to your letter. We deem it necessary for you to clarify the drawings that are in support of your proposal in order that we can finalise details, but in essence we are in favour of your proposal. From our records, there is no reason to think that your plans will interfere with any public or private access, and you therefore do not need to seek further advice from the Highways Agency.

To proceed, we require that you provide us with the architect's plans for your proposed extension **within 14 days**. These plans will then be checked before we are able to come to a final decision and possibly issue a ticket of certification.

Please send your plans marked for the attention of **The Planning Department**.

Yours sincerely,

P Lanning

1 Which department were the plans sent to? Choose **one** answer from the options below. (1 mark)

Planning Department   **Education Department**

County Hall Department   **Bart Terrace**

2 Does approval need to be sought from the Highways Agency? Explain your answer. (2 marks)

Test yourself

3 Who is the author of the original letter? Choose **one** answer from the options below. (1 mark)

Mr Hall   **P Lanning**   **Mr Grieves**   **Mudgeley**

4 What is meant by the word 'proceed' in the third paragraph? Choose **one** answer from the options below. (1 mark)

prevent   **continue**   **start**   **help**

5 Has the Planning Department definitely agreed to the extension? Explain your answer fully using evidence from the text. (2 marks)

Challenge yourself

6 Summarise why the Planning Department's response was delayed. (2 marks)

7 Summarise what needs to happen next. (2 marks)

How did you do?

Should children be allowed to use computers and the Internet?

The computer is a vital tool in today's world. It is useful in a huge number of ways and has contributed massively to the standard of living we now expect. Children enjoy using this technology, be it games consoles, tablets, phones or computers; they appear to be spending more time using this technology than on other things. The question remains as to whether the benefits children gain outweigh the dangers associated with them.

On the one hand, children can learn a huge amount of things from computers and the Internet. They learn about the wider world and can play games that help them with educational studies, such as reading and writing. New initiatives that allow children to read books online and answer questions to demonstrate their understanding further add to the argument regarding the benefits of technology. Children are able to access a wealth of information for school projects and save this information in order to present in different ways. The Internet allows children to connect with others that are further away and therefore learn about global matters. Using tablets for things like 'Facetime' allows children to stay in touch with friends and family. In essence, computers allow children to be global citizens; something books cannot do on their own.

On the other hand, computers can be a negative influence on children's lives. They allow children to see bad things meant for older people, such as videos and accessing chat rooms. This can result in children being drawn into a dangerous online world that their parents and teachers do not know about. Another very worrying side effect of using technology is children are forgetting how to 'play'. Instead of running in the fields, meeting up with friends, climbing trees and learning sports, children sit in their rooms playing on their technology. So although they might be global citizens, they are not spending as much time with their families and friends.

Therefore, there are both good and bad points to children using computers and the Internet. If parents take care and supervise their children, limiting the time they spend and checking that they are safe, then this type of technology can really enhance a child's life.

1 From this article, what can computers help children improve? Write down **one** answer. (1 mark)

2 What type of text is this? Choose **one** answer from the options below. Explain your answer. (2 marks)

recount   **explanation**   **discussion**   **instruction**

3 Write **one** benefit of children having access to the Internet and computers. (1 mark)

4 Write **one** disadvantage to children having access to the Internet and computers. (1 mark)

5 Write the word that shows computers are definitely needed in today's world. (1 mark)

6 'Books are less dangerous than information on the Internet'. Explain this sentence, using information from the text. (2 marks)

7 Write a summary sentence to show the purpose of each of the four paragraphs in the text. The first one has been done for you. (2 marks)

Paragraph 1 = To introduce the topic to the reader.

8 Explain the following sentence using information from the text. (2 marks)

Children who use the Internet are good global citizens but not good local citizens.

9 Does the author of the text think children should be allowed to use computers? Explain your answer. (3 marks)

10 Do you think children should be allowed to use computers and the Internet? Explain your answer. (3 marks)

Score ⬤ / 18

43

Acknowledgements

The author and publisher are grateful to the copyright holders for permission to use quoted materials and images.

Page 8 from *The Case of the Missing Stamp* from 20 Mini Mysteries by Dina Anastasio, originally published by Scholastic Children's Books 1989, copyright © Dina Anastasio.

Page 12 from *Journey to Jo'burg* by Beverley Naidoo, reproduced by permission of The Agency (London) Ltd © Beverley Naidoo; all rights reserved and enquiries to The Agency (London) Ltd, 24 Pottery Lane, Holland Park, London W11 4LZ.

Page 16 from *Matilda* by Roald Dahl, published by Jonathan Cape & Penguin Books Ltd.

Published by Keen Kite Books
An imprint of HarperCollins*Publishers* Ltd
1 London Bridge Street
London SE1 9GF

ISBN 9780008161736

First published in 2015

10 9 8 7 6 5 4 3 2 1

Text and design © 2015 Keen Kite Books, an imprint of HarperCollins*Publishers* Ltd

Author: Rachel Axten-Higgs

The author asserts his moral right to be identified as the author of this work.

All rights reserved. No part of this publication may be reproduced, stored in a retrieval system, or transmitted, in any form or by any means, electronic, mechanical, photocopying, recording or otherwise, without the prior permission of Keen Kite Books.

Series Concept and Commissioning: Michelle I'Anson
Series Editor and Development: Shelley Teasdale
Inside Concept Design: Paul Oates
Project Manager: Jane Moody
Cover Design: Carolyn Gibson
Text Design and Layout: Q2A Media
Production: Niccolò de Bianchi
Printed in Great Britain by Martins the Printers, Berwick upon Tweed

A CIP record of this book is available from the British Library.

Images are ©Shutterstock.com